Every innovation in Islam is misguidance. Al-Hadith

BIDAH

(INNOVATING) IN ISLAM IS A WAY TO GET LOST (OF IMAN)

Sheik Abdurrahmaan al-Sheha

Bidah
(Innovating) in Islam is a way to get lost of Iman

By
Sheik Abdurrahmaan al-Sheha

Translated by
Mufti Ahmad

In the Name of Allah, He is the Most Merciful, the Most Compassionate

Author's Note

Islam is a perfect religion, it has been strictly forbidden to mix innovation in Islam.

In this book the writer has tried to explain that when innovation is added to Islam, how many rotation issues are born, which are very dangerous for faith and Islam.

Table of Contents

Author's Note 4
Terminology used in this book 7
Introduction 9
Is the Din of Islam complete? 21
The opinion on adding something to the Din 24
What is Bid'ah? 28
Bid'ah's categories and innovations in religion 32
Religious innovations can be classified into three categories: 34
What does the Shari'ah say regarding innovations? 37
Scholars' Opinion on Bid'ah 41
Some evidence justifying Bidiah 44
Our opinion about the people who make Bid'ah 49
The individual who performs Bidiah: 49
The act of Bidíah: 50
The reasons for the spread of Bid'ah 51
The conditions for the acceptance of good plays 61
1. The reason for the act of worship: 62
2. The type of act: 62
3. The procedures: 63

4. The method: 63
5. The moment it is performed: 64
6. The place: 64
The dangers of doing Bid'ah: 64
Warning and reprimand 67
Glossary 71

Terminology used in this book

1. Rab: Some prefer to translate the term "Rab" as Lord. Apart from this being a biblical term that refers to the supposed lordship of the servant of God, the Prophet Jesus, the word "Lord" is limited to "master", "head", "owner" or "ruler" and does not suffice to express the meaning of "Rabbi". Among other meanings, ìRabî means the Creator, Who gives form, the Provider, on Whom depends the sustenance of all creatures, and the only one who gives life and causes death.

2. Din: The word translated as religion is "Din", which in Arabic refers to a way of life, both private and public. It is a broad term that includes severalthings: acts of worship, political practice, and a detailed code of conduct that includes behavioral and hygiene manners.

3. Sal'lal'laaho a'laihi wa sal'lam. Some translate it as "peace be upon". This translation is incorrect; the correct translation is: "may God exalt mention of him, and free him and his family from anything derogatory", but simply for a practical reason abbreviated • (P and B).

Introduction

All praises are to God, Whom I implore for help, and Whose forgiveness, guidance and protection against our own wickedness and sinful acts we seek. The one whom God guides along the straight path, cannot be diverted, nor can he be led by another but by… him. I bear witness that there is no other god worth worshiping more than God, One and, Who has no partners, and I testify that Muhammad (P and B) is the Servant and Messenger of God. May God exalt His Prophet (P and B), his family, his companions and those who follow the right path and away from all evil, and grant them safety on the Day of Resurrection.

Matters related to Din must be accepted without the slightest doubt. God, the Exalted, says in the Holy Quran:

> "The precepts that the Messenger has transmitted to you, respect them, and abstain from what has been prohibited. And fear God, for God is severe in punishment".(59: 7)

10 Bidah (Innovating) in Islam is a way to get lost

We must follow the guidance of the Prophet (P&B) on these matters, and we cannot do ijtihaad, that is, exert his efforts to pass judgment, on a matter that does not allow it. God the Exalted says:

> "Say, If you turly love God, Follow me! And god will love you and forgive you your sins. And God is absolving, merciful".(3:31)

A Prophet Muhammad (P and B) said:

> One of the things that nulifies our iman (faith) is not following his guidence".

He said:

> "You will not be true believers until your wishes are not in accordance with what I have been sent." (Broadcast by Baihaqi)

Muslims should refrain from making false claims as part of the religion, as this would divert them from the right path, and eventually lead them to Hell. The Prophet (P and B) said:

> "Whoever innovates in our Din, something alien to it, will be rejected". (Broadcast by Bukhari)

Many who call themselves Muslims perform acts of worship that contradict the teachings of Islam or practice certain innovative rites that are not based on the Din of God but follow his whims and desires. God condemned these people when He said:

> "Do you think, O Muhammad, that you can watch over the works of those who do everything that their passions dictate". (25:43)

If the dangers of practicing these new rites were confined to the individual only, the matter would not be so serious, despite not recognizing it. In reality, innovations negatively influence all Muslims, because out of ignorance, many may approve and agree with these practices or may sumpathize with those who do.

12 Bidah (Innovating) in Islam is a way to get lost

The innovations that are added to the Din lead to the deterioration of the life of the Muslims and separate them rom god. Furthermore, the innovations negatively influence non Muslims because seeing people claiming to be Muslims engaging in Illogical practices and behaving irrationally contradicing the spirit of Islam, They will feel rejection of Islam and thisk that it is like any other religión that is base don false and illogical beliefs.

We can classify the people who practice innovations into three categories:

First category: People who innovate because of their ignorance of Din matters. Islam does not excuse these people, as the solution to this problem is to ask. No one can practice worship according to his whims. God says:

> "Ask the knowledgeable people from among the People of the Book if you dont know". (21: 7)

People who innovate blindly following the example of their

predecessors are also part of this category. God says in the Holy Quran:

> "And when they are told: Follow what God has revealed, they respond: We follow the tradition of our fathers. Are you still following them when Satan seduced them taking them to the road that she drives to fire from Hell".(31:21)

Because the Practice types of innovations contradict the Shari'ah (Islamic jurisprudence), they make these people deviant and what they do does not benefit them. Following a few acts of worship according to the Sunnah of the Prophet (P&B) is better and more rewarding than doing many innovative practices. God says:

> "Sofocado for the punishment, beintroduced in the Intense fire." (88: 3-4)

Second category: People who seek material gain benefit from people's ignorance to achieve their goals. These types of people are further removed from Din and some even falsely call themselves Muslims, when in reality they have nothing of Islam. They distort and spoil the image of Islam with their innovations. The Prophet (P and B) said:

> "The worst servant is one who seeks to obtain material gain by performing practices that should be sincerely performed by and for God; the worst servant is the one who sticks to doubtful matters and makes lawful what is unlawful". (Broadcast by Hakim)

Third category: They are the enemies of Islam and do everything possible to spread religious innovations to divide Muslims. These people financially support those who innovate in religion to create new sects that contradict the beliefs of Ahlus-Sunnah wal-Jama'ah.

In this way, the enemies of Islam will achieve their main objective of alienting Mulims from their Aquidah and their Din no matter how slight.

Innovating in Dini s one of the methods satan uses to mislead people.

Ibn Abíbas said about the exegesis of God's words:

> "And (their leaders) said: Do not abandon our idols. Do not abandon Wad, Suua, Yaguz, Iauq and Nasrî".(71:23)

These are names of pious men of the people who lived in the time of NoÈ; When they died, Satan s incited them to raise figures in the places where they lived so that they would be remembered, and they gave them their names, but they were not worshiped until they died and were forgotten.

Imam Ibn al-Qayyim said: Satan tries to destroy Adam's son in seven stages. Some are more intense than others. Satan will not try to destroy you in the next phase until you have failed in the previous phase. These stages are:

First stage: The stage when you stop believing in God, in His Din, in His Perfect attributes, in what the Prophet (P and B) has said and in the promise that we will be resurrected. If Satan succeeds in misleading the believer at this stage, his enmity with him lessens and he rests for a time. If the believer passes this test and survives this stage, Satan will try to destroy him in the next stage.

Second stage: It is the stage of Bidiah (innovation in religion), either by believing in something other than the truth with which the Messenger (P and B) was sent or by worshiping others besides God, such as idols or images. Satan s relishes when the believer succumbs at this stage, because Bidiah comes into conflict with Din and leads him to reject it. In addition, those who make innovations in religion do not regret their actions but also invite others to do the same.

By making innovations in religion, a person fabricates lies against God and speaks without knowing, thus openly contradicting the Sunnah. Starting by practicing a few innovations will lead to major innovations in the future and thus the person will eventually turn away from Islam.

Scholars and scholars know well about the real dangers of

17 Bidah (Innovating) in Islam is a way to get lost

practicing Bidiah. If a person is successful and survives this stage, adhering to the Sunnah, and understanding its texts as the godly predecessors did, then Satan will seek to destroy him in the next stage.

Third stage: It is the stage of grave sins. If Satan is able to destroy the believer at this stage, he will consecrate the action he is taking and probably force him to say: No sin will harm the Tawhid (the creed) in the same way as no good It works to benefit the one who has committed Shirk (that is, to associate partners in the worship of God) î. If the person is successful and survives in this stage, Satan will seek to destroy him in the next stage.

Fourth stage: The stage of minor sins. Satan will force the person to minimize these sins and whisper to him: Fear not, as long as you do not commit major sinsÖ øDon't you know that minor sins are atoned for by moving away from more serious ones? î. In this way, Satan convinces the individual that it is not wrong to commit minor sins so that he continues to act in this way and begins to commit them on a regular basis. The person who has committed a serious sin, and has sincerely repented and is ashamed of what he has done, is better than that; because committing minor sins regularly is in itself a serious sin. Constant repentance removes major sins, and likewise, no minor sin is minor if it is committed constantly. The Prophet (P and B) said:

> "Fear for minor sins; They are like people who stop in the valley, they go in search of firewood to light the fire and each one brings a twig; they were able to light the fire and they were able to cook their bread. Whenever a person frequently commits a lesser sin, they will end up "destroyed". (Broadcast by Ahmed)

If the believer is successful and survives this stage by being careful, constantly repenting before God, and doing good works, Satan will seek to destroy him in the next stage.

Fifth stage: Satan lures the individual to be excessively lenient with the lawful things of religion to separate him from the worship of God. In this way, Satan tries to get the believer to abandon the practice of the Sunnah, and later to abandon the obligatory practices.

The believer succeeds and survives in this stage, realizing the greatness of the acts of worship, Satan will seek to destroy him in the next stage.

Sixth stage: It is the stage in which the believer spends his time doing works that do not have great reward. Satan encourages him to perform certain acts and beautifies them to make the individual believe that he has a great reward for them and thus keeps him from doing better and more beneficial works. When Satan fails to mislead the believer, he tries to make him at least receive fewer rewards, thereby entertaining him with unimportant works.

Seventh stage If Satan fails in the previous stages, then he will try to harm the person in any way possible, invoking his men and followers to act against the individual. The Prophets and Messengers were not safe from this. One must wait patiently because victory and success are linked to patience.

The worst outcome of Bidiah is making up lies about the Prophet (P and B). The Prophet Muhammad (P&B) considered this a very serious sin. He said:

> "Inventing a lie about myself is not the same as inventing a lie about anyone; Whoever lies about me has his seat assured in Hell". (Broadcast by Bukhari)

The Prophet's partner, Abdullah bin Masud, said:

> "Follow the guidance of the Prophet (P and B) and do not innovate because you have already been satisfied."

What wonderful words Abdullah bin Masud spoke! Any intellectual should think of these words. Certainly the sayings, actions and everything that the Prophet (P and B) approved is sufficient for a person in all respects and there is no reason for him to perform Bidiah.

The Prophet (P and B) said:

> "A work must be carried out with excessive eagerness for a period of time. So those who follow my Sunnah eagerly will be well guided, and whoever follows otherwise will be destroyed". (Reported by Ibn Khuzaimah)

Is the Din of Islam complete?

It is known that necessarily the Din of Islam is complete, according to the words of God Almighty, when he said:

> "Today I have perfected your religion for you, I have completed My grace upon you and I have arranged for Islam to be your religion". (5: 3)

Islam encompasses all aspects of the human being in this life and in the Hereafter. God says:

> "We have revealed to you the Book that contains all the precepts (that men need) and which is a guide, mercy and

joy for those who submit to God". (16:89)

Any aspect of the Shari'ah that has not been clarified in the first source of Islamic Law, which is the Qur'an, has been clarified in the second source of Islamic Law, which is the Sunnah. The Sunnah includes the sayings of the Prophet (P and B), his actions and everything that he approved of, but it must have been transmitted by a solid chain of narrators to be reliable. God says:

> "We send them with clear evidence and with the Books. And we reveal the Qur'an to you so that you can explain its precepts to men, and thus you will reflect". (16:44)

The Prophet (P and B) clarified and demonstrated to his people all the good and warned them about all the bad. The Prophet said:

> "There was no Prophet before me, except for what was incumbent upon them, who clarified to his people the good they knew and warned them about the evil they knew." (Reported by Muslim)

23 Bidah (Innovating) in Islam is a way to get lost

Those who believe otherwise certainly do not believe in the Qur'an which has been revealed to the Prophet (P and B). Whoever makes innovations in the Din believes that the Din of God is incomplete, and considers that he is completing it with his innovations.

The Muslim who innovates in religion, in fact, blames the Prophet (P and B) for not having delivered the message that was entrusted to him. Basically, it means: "Islam needs this innovation that the Prophet (P and B) overlooked, so it will complete the Din with this innovation."

The Prophet (P and B) said:

> "I have left a clear path for you, his night is like his day and no one will depart from him except by those who will be destroyed". (Broadcast by Hakim)

........*

The opinion on adding something to the Din

God, Exalted be He, says in the Holy Quran:

> "It is not like that, those who surrender to God and are benefactors will have their reward with their Lord, and they will not fear or be sad." (2: 112)

This means that those who sincerely practice religion for God and act according to the Sunnah of the Prophet (P and B), will be the only ones who will enter Paradise.

Imam Ahmed, may God have mercy on his soul, narrated that Abdullah bin Masud said: ìThe Prophet (P and B) drew a line and he said: ëThis is the way of Godí, and then he drew several small lines next to the big line and said: ëThese are ways, and in each way there is Satan who calls peopleí. Then he recited God's words:

> "And this is my straight path, follow it then. And you do not follow other paths, because if you do, they will divide you and deviate from His path. This is what He has ordered you to fear Him". (6: 153) (Reported by Ibn

Hibíban)

The Prophet (P and B) also said:

> "Certainly the most truthful of sayings is the Book of God and the best guide is the guide of Muhammad, and the most evil business is to innovate and every innovation in religion is Bidíah, and each Bidíah is way of detour that leads to Hell.(Reported by Ibn Khuzaimah)

The danger and importance of speaking without knowledge in matters of religion is clearly demonstrated in the Qur'an and in the sayings of the Prophet (P and B). God, Exalted be He, says:

> "To God belong the most sublime names and attributes, invoke Him with them. And separate yourselves from those who blaspheme with them and deny them; they will be punished for what they did". (7: 180)

He says:

> "Don't do or say anything if you don't have knowledge. By the way, you will be questioned about what you have used

your hearing, your sight and your heart on".(17:36)

And says:

> "Do they (idolaters) have accomplices (in unbelief) who have established religious precepts for them that God has not allowed". (42:21)

One who performs an act of innovation in the Din of God by legalizing something that is illegal or making something that is permitted illegal, will become an unbeliever if he does not repent, as the Prophet (P and B) explained about the God's words:

> "They took their rabbis and their monks as legislators instead of God." (9:31)

He said:

> "In spite of not worshiping them openly, but they consider lawful what their rabbis and monks made lawful, and they consider illegal what their rabbis and monks have considered ilegal". (Broadcast by Tirmidi)

27 Bidah (Innovating) in Islam is a way to get lost

This severe warning encompasses all who persist in proclaiming as lawful or unlawful what it is not.

The exegete Sheik Abdurrahman as-Saidi, may God have mercy on his soul, said:

> "The rabbis and monks enacted laws and dictates for their people that contradicted the Din of the Messengers and the people followed them. They used to magnify their Sheikhs and pious people, they considered them as gods apart from God, and they offered them animal sacrifices, they begged and begged them"

* * *

What is Bid'ah?

In order to understand the meaning of Bidiah, we must understand what the term Sunnah implies. Imam Ibn Rajab, may God have mercy on his soul, said: ìSunnah is a way to follow, it includes everything that the Prophet (P and B) and his well-guided Caliphs adhered to on creed, practice and beliefs. Sayings, this is the complete Sunnah.

Fulfilling and adhering to the Sunnah, whether in belief, actions or sayings is of great concern. God says:

> "There is a beautiful example in the Messenger of God (of courage and firmness in faith) for those who hope in God, (long to be rewarded) on the Day of Judgment and often remember God". (33:21)

The Prophet (P and B) also emphasized the importance of keeping his Sunnah. He said:

> "I recommend that you fear God and that you listen and obey, even if an Abyssinian (Ethiopian) slave has authority over you, because certainly those of you who live will

witness many differences. Therefore adhere to my Sunnah, and to the Sunnah of the well-guided Caliphs who will come after me. Stick firmly. Bite it with your teeth. Be very careful not to innovate. All innovations in religion are a detour and every detour leads to Hellfire". (Reported by ibn Hibban)

Ibn Taymiyyah, may God have mercy on his soul, said in his book Fatawa al-Kubra ([1]):

"Muhammad (P and B) has been sent to human beings and geniuses to clarify matters pertinent to Din, such as beliefs, goals of the Shari'ah and others. You will not accept · another Aquidah that is not yours and you will not accept · another Shariíah that is not yours. No one will approach God, nor obtain His pleasure, nor reach Paradise, unless they submit and strictly follow His sayings, actions, and beliefs, believe in the affairs of the unknown world, and perform acts of worship.,refraining from committing sins".

---

[1] pp. 178-179

Almighty God says:

> "Certainly sincere believers will not fear or grieve on Judgment Day." (10:62)

And says:

> "Oh, Humans! We have created you from a man (Adam) and a woman (Eve), and (from their descendants) we gather you into peoples and tribes so that you may knwo one another. Turly the most honored of you before God is the most merciful. Certainly God is Omniscient and well informed of what you are doing. (49:13)

Taqwa (Mercy) is achieved when an individual performs acts of worship in accordance with the Sunnah expecting to obtain God's reward, when he renounces disobeying God, and when he fears God's punishment. A wali (a pious person) does not reach this level until Complies with Fard (mandatory) acts and Nafl acts (Supererogatory).

God says:

"The most beloved thing for Me is when My servants approach ME, it is what I have commanded, and My servant continues to approach Me by performing supererogatory acts until I love him". (Broadcast by Bukhari)

Bidah: linguistically refers to an innovation, a novelty, something originated, or innovated that did not exist before. God, Exalted be He, says:

The *Ba'di*[2] of the heavens and the Earth, when he decides one thing, he says: Let it be! and it is. (2: 117)

Shaykh Abdurahman as-Saídi, may God have mercy on his soul, said:

"Baídi, the Originator and Creator, as what... he has created perfectly[3]. God says: "Oh Muhammad tell them: I

---

[2] Derived from the root of the word ba-dia'aa which means to originate.

[3] . *Taysir al-Karim ar-Rahman fi Tafsir Kalam al-Man'naan*

am not the first of the Messengers." (46: 9)

This means: I am not the first to come with God's message for humanity; but other Messengers have preceded me. And when they say: ëFulano de tal has performed Bidíahí, and it means that he has initiated a method that is unprecedented.

Bid'ah's categories and innovations in religion

We can classify the Bidiah into two categories:

First category: Bidiah in religion (innovations). This includes innovations in the Din of God, which contradict the guidance of our Prophet (P and B) and the path of the pious predecessors, whether on matters of belief or acts of worship. This type of Bidiah is considered illicit in the Qur'anic texts. God says:

> "Whoever departs from the Messenger after the guide has been shown to him, and follows a path other than that of the believers, we will abandon him and enter him into

---

Sheik as-Sa'di, may God have mercy on his soul; p. 725.

33 Bidah (Innovating) in Islam is a way to get lost

Hell. What a bad fate!" (4: 115)

The Prophet (P and B) said:

> "All my Ummah will enter Paradise, except whoever refuses to enter." They asked him: "Who will refuse to enter Paradise?" He replied: "Whoever obeys me will enter Paradise, and whoever disobeys me refuses to enter". (Broadcast by Bukhari)

Shaykh Islam bin Taymiyyah, may God have mercy on his soul, said:

> "That is why God, Exalted be He, has ordered us to say prayer at home:" Guide us on the straight path. The path of those whom you graced, not the path of the execrated or the lost yes (1: 6-7). Those who have earned the wrath of God are those who know the truth and oppose it, and those who have wandered are those who worship God without knowledge, while knowing that this is opposed to the Book

of God and the Sunnah [4].

Religious innovations can be classified into three categories:

1. The Bidiah that equates to disbelief, which alienates the believer from Islam; This type of Bidiah is related to matters of belief, such as offering animal sacrifices to others other than God, someone who circumnavigates a grave, someone who pleads with and seeks help from another other than God in matters other than God. they can help. God says:

> "Tell them: By the way, my prayer, my oblation, my life and my death belong to God, Lord of the Universe".(6: 162)

2. The Bidiah that does not equal disbelief, but it leads to unbelief, such as building structures over graves and praying or making supplications near them. That is why the Prophet (P and B) forbade his Ummah to visit his grave frequently for fear that they will worship him on the same

---

[4] Fatawa al-Kubra, p. 194

level as God. The Prophet said:

> "Do not transform your homes into graves (by not offering acts of worship within them) and do not visit my grave frequently and (do not burden yourself with the obligation to visit me) exalt my name, because it will come to me from where you are". (Broadcast by Abu Dawood)

The Bidiah that is the same as sins, such as celibacy, that is, avoiding marriage, fasting continuously and praying throughout the night. Anas narrated that the Prophet (P&B) said: "Three people went to the houses of the Prophet's wives and asked them about the worship performed by the Prophet (P&B). When they responded, they considered that it was not enough and said: "We are not like the Messenger of God, God has forgiven him of his past and future sins." One of them said: "I will never marry." The other said: "I will fast" and I will not break the fast. "The third said: "I will pray at night continuously". When the Prophet (P and B) heard this, he called them and said:

"Are you the ones who said this? Certainly i amwho most fears God of all of you and I am the most pious, yet I pray and sleep, fast and stop fasting, and marry women, so whoever does not follow my Sunnah is not one of us".(Broadcast by Bukhari)

From this example it is clear that whoever worships God in a way that God and His Messenger have not made lawful or that has been practiced by well-guided Caliphs, is a person who innovates in religion. The Prophet (P and B) said:

"I recommend that you fear God, and that you listen and obey, even if an Abyssinian (Ethiopian) slave has authority over you, because certainly those of you who live will be witnesses of many differences, therefore, adhere to my Sunnah, and the Sunnah of the well-guided Caliphs who will come after me. Stick firmly. Bite it with your teeth. Be very careful not to innovate. All innovations in religión...These are not called Bidiah, although they are considered as such from the linguistic point of view. The Prophet (P and B) did not warn us about this type of

Bidiah. All customs, worldly affairs, and business transactions are lawful, as long as they do not reach the point of becoming forbidden acts. This category is not considered a religious innovation because it is not related to acts of worship.

What does the Shari'ah say regarding innovations?

We must clarify that the second part of the Testimony of Faith, ìMuhammad is the Messenger of Godî, implies that the person obey him and faithfully believe in what he has transmitted and that he moves away from everything that he has prohibited. It also implies that the person must worship God in the way that He allowed and dictated, not in the way that each one wishes. Rejecting innovations is an obligation. God says in the Holy Quran:

> "And let those who disobey the orders of the Messenger of God (and reject his Message) be on the safe side, lest misfortune befall them or severe punishment strikes them". (24:63)

38 Bidah (Innovating) in Islam is a way to get lost

The Prophet (P and B) said:

> "Whoever innovates in our Din, something alien to it, will be rejected". (Broadcast by Bukhari)

Hudhaifah bin al-Yaman, may God have mercy on his soul, said: People asked the Messenger of God (P and B) about the good and the good things, and I asked him about the evil, for fear of being a witness of that kind of thing. I said: "Oh, Messenger of God, in the past we lived in ignorance, and God guided us with this goodness, then" will there be some evil after this goodness? Said yes. He asked: Will there be any good after that evil? He said: "Yes, after certain trials and tribulationsí. He asked: What kind of trials and tribulations? He said: People who follow something other than my Sunnah, and guide her, will recognize some of her practices and not be familiar with others. I asked him: Will there be any evil after that goodness? He said: Yes, those who invite to enter the gate of Hell, whoever answers them will be thrown into Fuegoí. I said, "Oh, Messenger of God, what should I do if I witness this? He told me: Hold on to the general assembly of Muslims and their Imami. I said: What will I do if there is no general assembly of Muslims and there is no Imam? He told me: "Give up all groups and fractions, even if you must hold on to a tree branch until death comes to you." (Broadcast by Bukhari)

Abdullah bin Masud, may God be pleased with him, narrated that the Messenger of God (P and B) said:

> "I will be the first to be near the Hawdh9 and people will arrive · and they will be forbidden · to drink and I will say: ë ° My Lord, my companions! í. And they will say: "You don't know what they have done after you." (Broadcast by Bukhari)

Abdullah bin Abbas, may God be pleased with him, narrated that God's Messenger (P and B) said:

> "God will not accept the works of a man who performs Bidiah until he abandons his practice".

40 Bidah (Innovating) in Islam is a way to get lost

(Transmitted by Ibn Mayah)

The Prophet (P and B) has informed us that there will be a great Fitnah (judgment and tribulation) to take place after him. The way a person will be safe at that moment to be adhering to the Book of God and the Sunnah of His Messenger (P and B). A person will not be safe if he makes innovations in religion.

Ali, may God be pleased with him, narrated that the Prophet of God (P and B) said:

> "There will be Fitnah. I said, "How can we protect ourselves from that?" He said: The Book of God has stories of your predecessors and joys of the things that will happen in the future, and explains how people should judge each other, and is the criterion to follow; Any ruler who neglects it, God will humiliate them · and take away · their pride. Whoever seeks guidance from another source, God will mislead him and that is God's firm noose, and it is a decisive reminder and the Straight Path. A person will

not be lost by his whims if he follows it correctly, nor will his recitation bring any doubt, his wonders will never cease to exist, the scholars still do not know enough, this caused the geniuses to reflect and ask: Certainly we have heard a wonderful Qur'an, which calls the guide. Whoever recites it, recites the truth, and whoever acts according to it will receive the reward. He who rules with him will do so with justice, and whoever invites others to him will be guided by the Right Path.(Broadcast by Tirmidi)

Scholars' Opinion on Bid'ah

Umar bin al-Khatab said: ìBe careful of people who adhere to their opinions and despise real evidence, because they are the enemies of the Sunnah; They cannot learn, memorize or understand the sayings of the Prophet (P and B), so they will continue to hold on to their opinions and that will lead them and others to go astray ".[5]

Ibn Abbas said about the words of God (3: 106):

---

[5]. Fath al-Bari 13/302

The Day of the I judge some faces will be radiant. They will be the Ahlus-Sunnah wal-Jama'ah and the people of knowledge. and others who are shadowed, are those who practice Bidiah and bad guidance. [6]

Omar bin Abdul-Aziz, may God have mercy on his soul, said: "The Messenger of God (P and B) established the practice of the Sunnah and his well-guided Caliphs continued the Sunnah. By doing so, they demonstrated the extent to which they sincerely believed in the Book of God, their absolute will to obey God, and the strength of the Din of God. No one can distort or change the Sunnah, or do anything that opposes it. Whoever follows this path will be well guided, and whoever seeks God's victory through the Sunnah will be victorious. Whoever opposes or contradicts the Sunnah and follows a path other than that of the believers, God will keep them · on the path they have chosen and burn · in Hell.

---

[6] . Usul al-I'tiqad 1/72

43 Bidah (Innovating) in Islam is a way to get lost

What a terrible abode!

Al-Fudail bin Aíyaad, may God have mercy on his soul, said: ìIf you see a man in the street doing Bidiah, take another path. God will not accept · any work done by one who makes innovations in religion, and whoever helps him, will certainly have · helped to destroy Islam [7].

Imam Sufian az-Zori, may God have mercy on him, said:

> Satan rejoices when a person makes innovations in religion more than when he commits some sin, because he can atone for his sins by repenting before God but at the same time. Doing Bidíah is not enough to just repent.

Imam Ibn al-Qayyim, may God have mercy on his soul, said:

> "If a heart is busy doing Bidiah, that person will stop practicing Sunnah."

---

[7] . Talbis iblis, p. 14

Some evidence justifying Bidiah

First test: Those who have little knowledge of the Shariah say that the words of the Prophet (P and B):

> "He who revive a good Sunnah practice in Islam, receive the reward for it and the corresponding reward for making others practice it; while those who practice it will not diminish its rewards. Whoever makes innovations in the practice of Islam, will receive the punishment for his sin and for the sin of those who practice it, and these sins will not diminish. (Reported by Muslim)

Rebuttal: The Prophet (P and B) said:

> "All Bidiah is a way of getting lost."

It is impossible for the Prophet (P&B) to have said something that contradicts something else he has said. Scholars agree with this unanimously.

To clarify this point, the Prophet (P and B) said:

> "Whoever makes good Sunnah practice reborn in Islam". Bidiah is not part of Islam, furthermore, the Prophet (P

45 Bidah (Innovating) in Islam is a way to get lost

and B) described the Sunnah as a good thing, while innovations cannot be described in the same way. There is also a difference between "making the practice of Sunnah reborn" and "initiating and establishing a false practice of Bidiah".

The meaning of this saying of the Prophet (P and B) becomes even clearer when the context in which this Hadith was said is understood: a group of homeless people approached the Prophet (P and B), then the Prophet (P and B) told the rest of the people to bring them whatever they could. A man of the InsarsHe approached the Prophet (P&B) bringing a bag full of silver that was quite heavy and put it in front of the Prophet (P&B). The Prophet (P&B) was very happy and said:

> "The meaning of this saying of the Prophet (P and B) becomes even clearer when the context in which this Hadith was said is understood: a group of homeless people approached the Prophet (P and B), then the

Prophet (P and B) told the rest of the people to bring them whatever they could. A man of the InsarsHe approached the Prophet (P&B) bringing a bag full of silver that was quite heavy and put it in front of the Prophet (P&B). The Prophet (P&B) was very happy and said:

"Whoever makes a good practice of Sunnah reborn in Islam will receive its reward and the reward of those who practice it until the Day of Resurrection". (Broadcast by Ahmed)

Examples: If a scholar goes to a country where no one teaches the Qur'an or the Sunnah of the Prophet (P and B) and sits in a mosque to teach the people or sends someone else to teach the people. An example is also used by a person who goes to a country where men normally shave their beards and orders them to grow their beards, it is a way of enforcing the Sunnah. In this way you will receive the reward just like those who practice the example that he has given them.

The Messenger of God (P and B) said: "Trim your mustaches, and grow your beard to differentiate yourself from the polytheists." (Hadith agreed)

When a person grows his beard and invites others to do the same and they do, he will have given birth to the Sunnah. This Hadith does not refer to those who make innovations in religion, because all innovations are a way of getting lost. In this regard, the Prophet (P and B) said:

> "Be very careful not to make innovations in Din, because all innovation is Bidiah, and all Bidiah is a way of getting lost." (Broadcast by Tirmidi)

Second test: The words of Omar bin al-Jatab, may God be pleased with him:

Meaning: What good Bidíah is this!

Rebuttal: Omar, may God be pleased with him, said these words when he met with the people in the Tarawih (night prayer) led by an Imam. On that occasion he used the literal meaning of Bidiah, not the legal sense of the word. You have to think that the prayer of Tarawih has its origin in the Shariíah. Omar did not make any innovations in it, but rather revived the Sunnah of the Prophet (P and B). The Prophet (P&B) prayed with his companions for three nights and then stopped praying in congregation, because he feared that it would become an obligation for his people.

The Prophet (P and B) said: "I fear that it will become an obligation for you and you cannot fulfill it." (Broadcast by Bukhari)

The companions prayed Tarawih while the Prophet (P and B) lived, and continued to do so after his death. They prayed together in groups in the Prophet's Mosque. Omar, may Allah be pleased with him, gathered the people behind an Imam, so the Prophet (P and B) had feared that it would not happen again. The Shari'ah was completed with his death, therefore, nothing can be added, and that is why Omar said:

49 Bidah (Innovating) in Islam is a way to get lost

How good *Bidah* is this! .

Our opinion about the people who make Bid'ah

God, Exalted be He, said:

> "Follow what has been revealed to you by your Lord, and do not take any protector outside of... Him. ° How little reflection · is! ". (7: 3)

The individual who performs Bidiah:

The person who carries out Bidíah can be classified into two categories according to the type of innovation carried out:

First category: Whoever makes innovations or deviates out of ignorance but does not spread it among the people. This person must learn the truth to become aware that his actions and deeds are contrary to the Shari'ah.

Second category: Who makes innovations or deviates to follow their own desires and whims. This person must be reminded of God's severe punishment and the truth must be clarified in an intelligent and appropriate way. If he refuses to accept the truth and categorically persists in doing Bidiah, people should be warned about this person and his false practices so that they can avoid him.

The act of Bidíah:

If innovation equates to disbelief, then people have an obligation to boycott the person making it if they have already offered advice and refused to accept it.

If Bidiah is not an act of disbelief and boycotting the person who does, allows it to return to the Sunnah, then it must be boycotted. But if this does not benefit you, then it should not be boycotted, as that will further distance you from the Sunnah. Sincere advice should be offered in a good way. The Prophet (P and B) said:

> "It is not lawful for a Muslim to boycott his brother for more than three days." (Broadcast by Bukhari)

The pious predecessors, may God be pleased with them, clarified and refuted each Bidiah in the light of the Qur'an and Sunnah. This is not a task only for scholars, but for all Muslims to witness an innovation in the Din of God, which surely does not have a solid foundation in the Shari'ah. If the individual can clarify his error with the truth, he must, otherwise, he must turn to someone who has sufficient knowledge to clarify the issue at hand and the misconceptions that support the acts that lead to the loss.

The reasons for the spread of Bid'ah

1. Do not apply the Shariah of God and be content with anything else. God says in the Holy Quran:

2. Oh, believers! Obey God, obey the Messenger and those of you who have authority and knowledge. And if you disagree about a matter, refer it to the judgment of God and the Messenger, if you believe in God and in the Day of Judgment, because it is the preferable and the correct path". (4:59)

3. Do not apply the Sunnah of the Prophet (P and B) and

abandon it. The further a person moves away from the practice of the Sunnah, the closer he gets to the possibility of making innovations in religion. The Sunnah of the Prophet (P and B) is rich in actions, sayings and approvals. There is no need for anyone to add any innovations. The Prophet (P and B) said:

> "I have left you two things with which you will never deviate: the Book of God, and my Sunnah, both will endure until I find them in the Hawdh". (Broadcast by Hakim)

4. Do not apply or not reflect on the meanings of the Qur'an or use it as a means to obtain Blessings; and abandon the remembrance of God, and not want to learn the affairs of Din. God the Exalted says:

> "To those who turn away from the memory that the Merciful sent (the Qur'an) we will assign a demon to be his inseparable companion (and whisper evil to him)". (43:36)

5. Reject the truth and not accept it. God says:

"And when one of them is told: Fear God, his sinful pride takes hold of him. His retribution will be Hell ° What a terrible whereabouts!" (2: 206)

6. Name pseudo-scholars or sages. The Prophet (P and B) said:

"God does not take knowledge away from his servants directly. He does it by bringing the wise men together (when they die) until no wise man is left alive and the people take as ignorant leaders to consult him on matters, and they will give their Fatawa (religious verdicts) without knowledge, and that will make people are lost and they themselves will be lost". (Broadcast by Bukhari)

7. Seeking knowledge only in books without attending classes of people specialized in religion. There are those who say:

"So-and-so's Sheik is his book," that is, he only depends on books to gain knowledge, but thus his mistakes will be more than his successes.

Similarly, we must refrain from reading books that raise doubts. On one occasion, Omar bin al-Khattab was reading a letter given to him by the People of the Book, and the Prophet (P&B) got angry and said to him:

> "Are you not sure of your Din, O son of Jatab? I swear by the One who has my life in His hands, that I have brought you the Shariah that is clear and pure. You do not consult them on any matter, because they can inform you with the truth and you may not believe it, or they can inform you with falsehoods and you can believe them. For the One who has my life in His hands, if Moses were alive, he would have no choice but to follow me". (Broadcast by Ahmed)

7. Failure to disseminate correct information; as for example, if the specialists in religion kept away from the people, in silence and did not share the knowledge they possess. God the Exalted says:

> "Those who hide the evidence and the guide that we reveal

to men after having clarified them will be cursed by God and all creation. Except for those who repent, amend and openly declare what they hid. To these I will accept their repentance, because I am Forgiving, Merciful". (2: 159-160)

9. Extremism and fanaticism in Din. ... This is one of the reasons why innovations and Shirk (polytheism) spread among the people. The Prophet (P and B) said:

"Be careful not to commit extremism in religion, because certainly your ancestors were destroyed by their extremism in Din". (Reported by Ibn Hiban)

10. Not having enough capacity to deduce things from religious opinions. God the Exalted says:

"A true believer or a true believer must not, when God and His Messenger have ruled on a matter, act contrary; and know that whoever disobeys God and His Messenger will have evidently deviated". (33:36)

11. Follow your own whims and desires. God says:

"Do you not notice (Oh, Muhammad!) the one who follows

his passions as if they were a divinity? God decreed by His divine knowledge that he would go astray, and so He sealed his ears and his heart, and put a veil over his eyes (and he could not hear, see or understand the truth). No one will be able to guide you after God has misled you. Isn't he reconsidering? (45:23)

12. Imitate and follow the opinion of the people blindly in the affairs of Din, without relying on knowledge and proper guidance, rather than looking for the answer in God's Book and His Prophet's Sunnah (P and B). God says:

"And when they are told: Follow what God revealed, they argue: We follow the tradition of our fathers. øDo they imitate their parents even though they did not reason or follow the guide?" (2: 170)

13.To be made friend from bad persons have bad companies. God says:

"The wicked one will bite his own hands (lamenting) and say: I wish he had followed the path of the Messenger! Woe to me! I wish I had not taken as a friend the one who separated me from the Truth! Well, I walked away from the Message, after it was transmitted to me. Certainly Satan betrays man ". (25: 27-29)

14. Neither order the good nor prohibit the evil. God says:

"May there be among you those who summon the good, ordering the good and forbidding the evil. ... Those are the ones who will be successful". (3: 104)

The Prophet (P and B) said:

"No Prophet has been entrusted to a nation without having had helpers and assistance from his companions who applied the Sunnah of that Prophet. After them came people whose words were they contradicted with their actions and whose actions contradicted their orders. So whoever fights them with their hands is a believer, and whoeverFight them with your heart, you are a believer, and there is no Faith beyond that."

(Reported by Muslim)

15. Following dubious texts about Shariah that ordinary people do not understand. God says:

> "it is the One who has revealed the Book to you. It contains verses of explicit meaning that are the basis of the Book, and others of implicit meaning. Those of lost heart follow only those of implicit meaning in order to sow discord and misinterpret them, but only God knows their true meaning, and (also) those rooted in knowledge, who say: We believe in all of them equally, all They come from our Lord, but only those endowed with intellect are reconsidered". (3: 7)

16. Be lenient with al-Wala and al-Bara (love and hate for God) issues. This includes loving God's enemies because showing love for them will make them emulate. Abu Waqid al-Laizi, may God be pleased with him, said:

> "When the Prophet (P and B) conquered Mecca, we went out with him (before the battle with the Hawazin tribe) until we passed a tree called Dat Auwat where the

disbelievers were supplicating and making supplications. We said: ëOh Messenger of God, assign a Dat Auwat for us like the one they have. The Messenger of God (P and B) said:

"God is the Big! The Children of Israel asked Moses to give them a god similar to theirs. Certainly you are ignorant yes. And then the Messenger of God (P and B) said: "Certainly emulate and follow your ancestors".(Reported by Ibn Hiban)

17. Making an effort to reach an opinion or conclusion on matters that are not worthwhile, such as deducing things from textual evidence that are not relevant. We must also consider that there are hadeeths that are not authentic, but are invented sayings that one must be very careful not to spread or use them to prove anything.

There are also weak hadeeths. Some scholars have legalized themes using weak hadeeths to incite people to do good works, as long as these hadeeths are not used to establish acts of worship. The acts of worship are established by authentic hadeeths that have been truthfully narrated since the Prophet (P and B).

61 Bidah (Innovating) in Islam is a way to get lost

The conditions for the acceptance of good plays

The works of God's servants will not be accepted unless they meet two conditions:

First condition: Sincerity, that is, they are performed by God with sincerity. God says:

> "And they had been commanded (in their laws) to worship God sincerely, to be monotheistic, perform prayer, and pay Zakat, for" that is the true religión". (98: 5)

God, the Exalted, says in a Hadith Qudsi: [8]

> "I do not need partners. Whoever does an action associating someone other than Me, will abandon him and his Shirk (idolatry)". (Reported by Muslim)

Second condition: Follow the example of the Prophet (P and B), that is, perform the acts of worship in the same way that he did. This condition will not be met if six important points

---

[8] . *Hadith Qudsi*: Its meaning is God, while the words are from the Prophet (P and B).

are not considered:

1. The reason for the act of worship:

If a person worships God for any reason that is not recognized in the Shari'ah, his actions will be rejected as being considered as a form of innovation.

Example: There are those who perform acts of worship on the night of the 27th of the month of Rajab. They argue that the Prophet (P and B) made his Night Journey that night. Praying at night is a valid act of worship but that the beginning of this practice was that night, does not agree with the Shari'ah. With this point we can differentiate between the acts of Bidiah and the Sunnah.

2. The type of act:

The act of worship must be in accordance with the Shari'ah. If a person worships God through an act of worship that is not recognized in the Shariah, he will not be accepted.

Example: If a person sacrifices a horse during the month of Dul Hiya (the 12th month of the Islamic calendar). The sacrifice that this person makes will not be accepted because it contradicts the Shari'ah on this point, since animal sacrifices can only be made with camels, cows, goats or lambs.

3. The procedures:

If a person wants to perform a prayer at any time considering it an obligatory prayer, he will not be accepted as such, since obligatory prayers are well known in the Shari'ah. Similarly, if a person prays the Duhr (the noon prayer) by performing five Rakats (units) instead of four properly, he will not be accepted.

4. The method:

If the person performs ablution and washes his feet and then wet his head, it is considered null and void, since ablution has a certain sequence that cannot be changed.

5. The moment it is performed:

If a person sacrifices an animal on the first day of the month of Dul Hiya, his sacrifice will not be accepted because he did not perform it on the corresponding day.

6. The place:

If a person does Iítikaf (stay in prayer) in another place than in a mosque, his Iítikaf is not correct since it is a requirement that it be done inside a mosque.[9]

The dangers of doing Bid'ah:

There is immense danger in doing acts of innovation; enemies of Islam can attack Muslims and their religion for that reason. All Muslims must be very careful that this is not used to harm the Din or the Muslims in any way. A Muslim should not cover up or hide an individual who makes innovations.

---

[9]. *Al-Ib'daa fi Kamaal ash-Shar* written by Sheik Muhammad bin Uzaimin.

65 Bidah (Innovating) in Islam is a way to get lost

The enemies of Islam have been able to divide Muslims with these innovations. Every time an innovation is spread, an act of the Sunnah is abandoned. Continually performing acts of innovation in religion will lead the believer to abandon the Din of God altogether. The Prophet (P and B) said:

> "My Ummah (the Muslims) will become divided into seventy-three sects, the sect with the largest number of adherents will be · whose members give precedence to their intellect and make analogies to make lawful the illicit and illicit the lawful". (Broadcast by Hakim)

Therefore, a person must make sure that all the acts of worship that he wants to perform do not contradict the Shariah. Everything that is congruent must be accepted, and what is not, must be rejected. The Prophet (P and B) said:

> "I have left you two things that you will never deviate with: the Book of God, and my Sunnah, both will endure until I find them in the Hawdh on the Day of Resurrection." (Broadcast by Hakim)

In order for a person to be safe, he must refrain from doing anything that contradicts the Book of God and the Sunnah of the Prophet (P and B).

The Prophet (P and B) said:

> Inventing a lie about myself is not the same as inventing a lie about anyone; Whoever lies about me has his seat assured in Hell. (Broadcast by Bukhari)

Whoever wants to be successful, and only expects God's reward, should follow the example of the Prophet (P and B). God, the Exalted, says in the Holy Quran:

> "Say: If you truly love God, follow me! And God will love you and forgive you your sins. God is Absolving, Merciful". (3:31)

A person should not emulate or follow another individual because human beings are not infallible, they are liable to make mistakes, you have worldly desires and can be guided by their whims.

Warning and reprimand

Abdulla ibn ad-Dailami said:

> "I have heard that the Din will divide · and go astray · by leaving the Sunnah." People will give up the practice of the Sunnah little by little, just as a rope becomes weaker and weaker over time". (Ad-DarimiNy 98)

Each of us should adhere to the Sunnah of the Prophet (P and B) and try by all means to spread its practice among the people and apply it. Goodness can be anticipated only when one applies the Sunnah of the Prophet (P and B) whether the Sunnah is a saying or an action, and when one rejects all kinds of innovation in the Din of God. It is also our obligation to correctly advise anyone we know who is doing something that is opposed to the Shari'ah, and to clarify things well to have the honor of defending the Din of God. The Prophet (P and B) said:

> "Pass on even one verse from me and you will have no sin if you tell the stories of the Children of Israel, and whoever

invents a lie about me, will have a guaranteed seat in Hell". (Broadcast by Bukhari)

Eliminating all acts of innovation is a collective task of the community. The Prophet (P and B) said:

"Whoever of you sees a bad deed, let him change it with his hand, if he could not with his tongue and if he could not, then in his heart, and this is the weakest of faith".(Reported by Muslim)

A person should do Daíwah (spread Islam) and call others to follow God's way as God commands in the Qur'an when he says:

"Summon the path of your Lord with wisdom and beautiful words. Argue them in the best way. Your Lord knows well who is straying from His path and who is following the guidance". (16: 125)

Religious matters should not be taken for granted by everyone who claims to have knowledge and understanding of Islam. Din must be learned from those who are trustworthy with their Din, knowledge and piety. The Prophet (P and B) said:

> "Certainly the sages of Islam are the heirs of the Prophets. The Prophets did not leave a single Dinar or Dirham, but they left their knowledge, therefore, whoever takes it and learns it, will have received a part of a great inheritance". (Reported by Ibn Hiban)

We should also keep in mind the words of the Prophet (P and B) when he said:

> "Whoever calls others to the right path will receive a reward equal to the reward of those who followed him, and their rewards will not diminish. And whoever calls others to deviate from the right path, will receive the same sins of those who have followed him, and their sins will not diminish". (Reported by Muslim)

In the same way, whoever guides others to do evil and an innovation is a kind of evil - he will be told about his sins and the sins committed by those who follow him. The

Prophet (P and B) said:

> "Certainly the most truthful of sayings is the Book of God, and the best guide is the guide of Muhammad, and the most evil business is to innovate, and every innovation in religion is *Bidah*, and each Bidiah is a form of detour that leads to Hell". (Reported by Ibn Khuzaimah)

As we have mentioned previously, the danger and seriousness of innovating on the matters of the religion of God is evident, therefore, whoever wants to take an action, first check if that is accepted by the Shari'ah. If it is, then let him do it and lead others to do the same, but if he contradicts the Shari'ah, then he must abandon that action and warn others who want to do it.

* ..... * ..... *

Glossary

1. Aqidah: Belief.

2. Bid'ah: An innovation or novelty; in this book it refers to religious innovations.

3. Dinar & Dirham: Types of coins from the time of the Prophet (P and B).

4. Faridah: An obligatory act of worship.

5. Fitnah: Judgment, conflict and tribulation.

6. Hadeeth: The tradition prophetic.

7. Hawdh: The source of water that God guaranteed to the Prophet (P and B), who drinks from it only once, will never be thirsty again.

8. Hudud: Severe punishments in Islam.

9. Hukum: Regulation.

10. Iytihaad: In general, it is to make a great effort. In this book it refers to the effort that each one makes to reach an agreement on a particular issue.

11. Itikaf: In general, it means to seclude oneself in prayer.

Iítikaf is an act of worship in which a person secludes himself in a mosque to worship God.

12. Magnet: Faith.

13. Jannah: It is the Abode in Paradise or the Paradise Gardens that God has guaranteed to his pious servants for Eternal Life. It is commonly translated as Paradise.

14. Kufr: Incredulous.

15. Nafl: Supererogatory Acts of Worship.

16. Shaitan: Satan · s.

17. Shari'ah: Islamic law and jurisprudence.

18. Shirk: Associate partners with God.

19. Sunnah: Has more than one meaning. You may refer to:

*.The tradition Prophetic.

*. The dicta · menes; that is, what determines that an act belongs to the Sunnah.

20. Tarawih: The nightly prayer that takes place during the holy month of Ramadan (ninth month of the Islamic calendar)

21. Taqwah: Me

22. Ummah: Nation Muslim.

23. Wali Pious, righteous and God-fearing Muslims, who perform obligatory acts of worship and refrain from all wrongdoing.

…..…..*

Lightning Source UK Ltd.
Milton Keynes UK
UKHW020636100622
404229UK00006B/768